Aftermath

A Play

Rae Terence

Samuel French – London
New York – Sydney – Toronto – Hollywood

GW83828

CHARACTERS

Vicar ⎫
John Ferris ⎬ Outsiders
Ellie ⎭
Regional Controller Evans ⎫
Captain Martin ⎬ Insiders
Doctor Henderson ⎭

Time—this year, next year, sometime

AUTHOR'S NOTE

Although divided into scenes the action is intended to be continuous, taking place in three separate acting areas which comprise the village graveyard, a room in John's house, and the office of the Regional Controller in the underground Regional Centre of Government. The settings may be as simple or elaborate as you wish.

In order to heighten the difference between life in the village and life in the Centre, I suggest that the "Outsiders" should have a dishevelled appearance and an exhausted manner, whereas the "Insiders" should be smartly dressed and be very alert. The part of Doctor Henderson may be played by either a man or woman.

AFTERMATH

The village graveyard, somewhere in south-west England

The vicar and John Ferris, a man of about forty, are standing in a pool of light. A burial service is just coming to an end

Vicar . . . we therefore commit her body to the ground; earth to earth, ashes to ashes, dust to dust; in sure and certain hope of the resurrection to eternal life through our Lord Jesus Christ; who shall change our vile body that it may be like unto his glorious body, according to the mighty working, whereby he is able to subdue all things to himself.

Pause

I heard a voice from heaven saying unto me, write: from henceforth blessed are the dead which die in the Lord; even so saith the Spirit for they rest from their labours.

Pause

Our Father which art in heaven . . . which art in . . . hallowed . . . (*He looks around helplessly, sighs and bows his head*) The grace of our Lord Jesus Christ and the love of God and the fellowship of the Holy Ghost be with us all evermore. Amen.

Pause

I'm truly sorry, John.

Pause

I shortened the service a bit, it seemed to be for the best. I hope you didn't mine?

There is no response

I know it's difficult to understand why these things have

happened, but we hold on to our belief in the infinite goodness and mercy of God, otherwise we are left with nothing. Don't you agree?

John She was only seven, you know . . . bright eyed . . . like a little bird . . . but all the birds have gone . . . only seven.

Vicar I know . . . John, I wish there was some comfort I could bring you.

John It doesn't matter, Vicar . . . nothing matters any more.

Vicar Don't say that! Not you! Listen, John. The only thing that has held this community together for these past three weeks has been your strength of will, you must not fail them now.

John Fail them . . .? Three weeks ago there were one hundred of us. What is it today? The last figure I heard was forty-three. What do you imagine it will be next week? There probably won't be anyone left.

Vicar But while they still have hope . . .

John There is no hope.

Vicar There is always hope, John.

John In that grave lies my seven year old daughter. Next to her lie my wife who we buried two days ago and my two other daughters who we buried last week. Have you forgotten how they died? Have you forgotten what I had to do? Don't talk to me about hope or belief.

Vicar God will forgive you for what you have done.

John God is dead! He ceased to exist on February the twenty-third.

Vicar No, John! God is not dead. He still loves and cares for his children.

John Then I swear this to you, Vicar—if God appeared before me in all his shining glory, I would strangle Him with my bare hands.

Vicar John!

John Leave me alone, Vicar.

Vicar I must try to make you——

John (*departing*) Leave me alone!

Vicar John, you mustn't deny your faith . . .

John exits

John . . .! (*Appealing to heaven*) Lord, help him in his grief, he must survive, without him there would be no hope . . . Our Father, which art in heaven, hallowed be Thy name, Thy kingdom——

Ellie enters. She is in her mid-thirties

Ellie Hello, Vicar. I see you're still keeping up the good work.
Vicar Ellie! When did you get back?
Ellie Just a few minutes ago.
Vicar Did you—did you find anybody else?
Ellie No.
Vicar But there must be others.
Ellie Not in the direction I went. I didn't see another living creature
... just dead cows, dead sheep, dead dogs, cats, birds,—and
people.
Vicar How far did you go?
Ellie Nearly as far as Exeter—about twenty miles—then I turned
round and came back ... drove the last few miles on a flat tyre ...
in the end the wheel fell off, so I walked the last couple of miles.
How are things here?
Vicar Not good. We buried five yesterday and four today so far ...
or was it four yesterday? I just can't keep track any longer. Dear
God, it must end soon.
Ellie Isn't this where John's wife and two daughters are buried?
Vicar Three daughters—the youngest one died this morning. I
can't even remember her name.
Ellie (*quietly*) Mandy, she was called Mandy.
Vicar Ah yes ... a pretty little thing. She was the last of all the
children. They've all gone now.
Ellie I suppose you and I were fortunate.
Vicar Fortunate?
Ellie Yes fortunate. You weren't married, and my husband and
kids were obliterated in the blink of an eyelid. John, poor devil,
has had to watch his family die.
Vicar (*quietly*) Not only watch.
Ellie And who's to blame him, Vicar? Not me, and not you. Well
I'd better go and report to him, although I've nothing to tell him
that he doesn't already know.
Vicar Ellie?
Ellie Yes?
Vicar It—it seems inconceivable that nobody else has survived.
Ellie All I know for certain, Vicar, is that the only living creatures
I've seen in the last few weeks are either in this village or
underground in the Regional Centre.

Vicar I wonder if those people in the Centre really have any idea of what it is like out here?

Ellie They'll find out, they can't stay in there for ever. Sooner or later they'll run out of food and water.

Vicar Be careful with John, he's had just about as much as he can take.

Ellie Haven't we all, Vicar, haven't we all?

Ellie exits

The vicar stands motionless, head bowed. The Lights fade slowly

SCENE 2

A room in John's house

The Lights come up on John, seated at a table with his head in his hands, a picture of utter dejection. There is a telephone on the table and a knapsack under the table. John takes a pistol out of his jacket pocket. He checks to see if it is loaded, holds it up and examines it, then puts the barrel against his forehead. The telephone rings loudly. John sighs, puts the pistol back in his pocket and picks up the receiver

John What do you want?

The Lights come up on the office in the underground Regional Centre of Government. Regional Controller Evans is sitting at a desk holding a telephone. Martin, an army captain of about thirty, stands beside him listening on an extension with his hand over the mouthpiece

Evans Ah, Ferris. Evans here.

John (*wearily*) It's Mr Ferris, and you don't need to tell me who you are, because nobody else calls these days.

Evans Er—yes—quite . . . Now see here, Ferris, you're over half an hour late with your report.

John Report?

Evans Yes, Ferris. Your daily report. This is the third day running I've had to chase you for it.

John I'm sorry. I had a personal matter to attend to.

Evans Well it's not good enough.

John I said I'm sorry. It's not as though it's of any bloody importance anyway.

Evans I'll be the judge of what is important and what isn't.

Captain Martin attracts his attention

Hang on a minute, Ferris. (*He puts his hand over the mouthpiece*)
What is it?

Martin He sounds just about at the end of his tether, sir. I don't
think we ought to push him too far.

Evans Must I remind you, Captain Martin, that you are here solely
as an adviser on security matters, and that I have complete
authority, both in this headquarters, and in this region?

Martin I'm not questioning your authority, sir.

Evans Then don't question my judgement either.

Martin It's just that we have no real idea of what it is like out there.
Conditions must be appalling.

Evans It's not exactly a bed of roses in here, is it? I've got far too
many problems to worry about without you going soft on me.

Martin I am not——

Evans Enough! Just let me handle this without any further
interruption. (*He removes his hand from the mouthpiece*) Hello,
Ferris. Are you still there?

John Where else would I be?

Pause

Evans (*impatiently*) Well?

John Well what?

Evans What have you got to report?

John (*sighing*) What do you want to know?

Evans I want a complete report on your situation.

John Our situation is exactly the same as it was yesterday, and the
day before that—except that a few more have died.

Evans I want some details on the deaths.

John What the hell for?

Evans I want a breakdown of male and female, adult and children
. . . and I also want to know how many died of radiation sickness
and how many died of—er . . .

John Yes?

Evans Er—how many died of other causes?

John There aren't any children left . . . the last one died this
morning.

Evans Oh . . . I'm sorry.

John (*angrily*) What makes you say that? You didn't know any of them.

Evans I'm not completely without——

John (*interrupting*) And as for your second question—we don't hold inquests out here any more ... when somebody dies we just bury them.

Pause

Evans How is the work progressing?

John Work?

Evans Don't be awkward with me, Ferris. The work—the preparation of the land for planting crops—how much has been done?

John (*sighing*) As I recall I don't think any has been done for the last couple of days.

Evans This isn't good enough, Ferris. When I put you in charge I told you that the preparation of the land was of paramount importance and took precedence over everything else. That instruction still stands. Do I make myself clear?

John We tend to have different priorities out here.

Evans I do not wish to resort to threats, but if you persist in disobeying my orders you will leave me no alternative.

John And what will you do from the safety of your bunker, mein Fuhrer?

Evans Unless you are prepared to co-operate fully I shall stop the issue of the daily food ration.

John What did you say?

Evans I believe you understood me.

John You jumped-up, never-come-down, brass-bound, stove-enamelled, bag of wind.

Evans How dare y——

John You can take your food rations and stuff them up your——

Evans Ferris!

John Sideways! (*He slams down the telephone receiver*)

The Lights fade quickly on John's room

Evans (*almost to himself*) Well ... Well!

Martin (*coughing*) I—er—I don't think he was too impressed by the threat, sir.

Evans Why on earth is he behaving this way? Surely he must realize that we have to pull together.

Martin When we spoke to him yesterday his youngest daughter was still alive . . . just now he said that the last of the children died this morning . . . it must have been her . . . (*Quietly*) I think I can understand his attitude.

Evans But we told him that it was unlikely that any of the children would survive.

Martin I doubt if that made it any easier.

Evans No. No you're quite right. Well, what are we going to do now?

Martin The radiation levels are just about down to normal. Some of us could go outside and complete the preparation of the ground for planting.

Evans (*sharply*) No!

Martin But——

Evans No! The directives are quite explicit. No-one must leave the centre before a minimum period of three months has expired.

Martin If we don't get the seed in before then we'll be too late. That means no fresh food for another twelve months. God knows what sort of health problems that may cause.

Evans We cannot disobey written orders. I wouldn't have thought that I'd need to explain that to you.

Martin Orders should only be followed blindly when the person who gave them is still around to modify them in the light of the prevailing circumstances. However, if you won't agree to anyone leaving the Centre, then all we can do is wait.

Evans Wait for what?

Martin To see if Ferris rings back.

The Lights fade slowly on the office

SCENE 3

A room in John's house

John is still seated at the table

Ellis enters carrying a bottle of whisky and two glasses

Ellie (*cheerfully imitating a fanfare*) Tarantara!

John Ellie!

Ellie puts the bottle and glasses on the table. She draws up another chair and sits down

Ellie Let us celebrate the return of the wanderer.

John Where on earth have you been?

Ellie starts to pour the whisky into the glasses

Ellie I went nearly as far as Exeter, then I made a slight detour to call on an elderly relative. After I'd given her a decent burial it was getting late so I spent the night there. I set off early this morning to miss all the traffic jams. (*She hands John a glass*) Cheers!

John (*wryly*) Cheers?

Ellie That, my friend, is one of the greatest whiskies ever made. You've got to say something when you drink it.

Ellie drinks, John does not

John (*quietly*) Mandy died this morning.

Ellie Yes ... Yes I know. I spoke to the vicar on the way here.

John About half an hour ago I was seriously considering suicide.

Ellie I wish I'd died with my family too. (*After a pause*) As a matter of interest, what stopped you?

John Would you believe Regional Controller Evans?

Ellie No!

John (*grinning*) It's true, he phoned just at the crucial moment.

Ellie pours herself another drink

Ellie I'm glad he did, otherwise I'd be sat here talking to myself. And what did our lord and master want?

John (*grinning*) My daily report — got a bit upset when I told him we'd not done any ploughing for a couple of days.

Ellie (*chuckling*) I wonder what he'd do if he knew that we hadn't done any ploughing at all?

John He's threatened very serious action.

Ellie (*laughing*) Such as?

John He's going to stop the daily food ration.

Ellie (*still laughing*) He's what?

John (*mimicking Evans*) I believe you understood me.

Ellie laughs louder still

(*Laughing*) I only used to collect the damn stuff because I thought it made him feel useful.

Ellie (*struggling to speak through her laughter*) Doesn't he realize we've got all the food in the south-west of England between a few dozen of us.

They are both now almost helpless with laughter when suddenly Ellie clutches her side gasping and moaning with pain

John Ellie! Oh God—Ellie, not you too?

Ellie I'm afraid so, John . . . I've—I've had a couple of attacks now . . . of course it could just be all the whisky I've been drinking . . . but I don't think so somehow. (*The pain is easing now*)

John Damn! DAMN!

Ellie Don't take it too badly, John. I'm a pretty boring sort of a person anyway. All I ask is that when the time comes you'll do the necessary.

John looks away, Ellie takes his hand

Please, John—it's the only comfort that's left to me.

John looks at her, then nods

Thanks. You know, my husband used to be a great believer in Spiritualism—used to go to all the meetings. I remember he once told me that when a person dies a violent and unexpected death then the spirit of that person suddenly finds itself on the other side without having the faintest idea about what has happened. As a consequence that spirit feels frightened, bewildered, angry, and very, very bitter. I remember I laughed at the time . . . (*She shivers*) . . . I swear to you, John, when I drove through that deserted countryside the air around me was solid with anger, and great waves of bitterness kept flooding around me, as if millions of souls were crying out "WHY?".

There is a pause. Then John comes to a decision. He picks up the telephone receiver and dials a single number

The Lights come up on Evans and Martin slumped in chairs at the desk in the office. The telephone on the desk rings

Evans Ah, it didn't take long for him to come to his senses.

The telephone rings again. Martin goes to pick it up but Evans stops him

Let him wait a while—we mustn't appear too eager

The telephone rings several more times

John Damn.
Ellie Don't tell me it's engaged.
John (*grinning*) No, it's ringing, but I think Evans is playing silly beggers.

Evans picks up the receiver, Martin picks up the extension

Evans Evans here.
John I think we'd better have a talk.

Evans gives a smile of self satisfaction to Martin

Evans I'm always ready to discuss any problems that you might have, that's why we provided you with a telephone.
John No, I don't mean a talk on the phone. I think it's about time we met.
Evans (*sharply*) That is completely out of the question—for the next few weeks at least.
John Well you please yourself, of course, but as soon as this conversation is over I shall destroy this phone.
Evans No! No don't do that—let's just talk this out.
John There's nothing to discuss. Make your mind up; yes or no?
Evans Hang on a minute. (*He puts hand over mouthpiece and speaks to Martin*) What do you think?
Martin Well, speaking solely as your security adviser, sir, I must advise against letting him into the Centre. However, as you won't go out of the Centre, he seems to have you over the proverbial barrel, and he knows it. If you want to keep some sort of relationship going then I think you'll have to see him.
Evans (*speaking into the telephone*) All right, Ferris. I agree to your request. I'm prepared to let you enter the Centre, but that is on the strict understanding that nobody else approaches nearer than fifty yards of the doors.
John Agreed.
Evans How soon can you be here?
John In about half an hour.

Ellie wags a finger at him and shakes the bottle, John grins

Better make that an hour. (*He replaces the receiver*)

The Lights fade on the office

He's getting almost amenable.

Ellie You've got to have some sympathy for the poor man. I bet he's got a stack of rules and regulations this high and nobody to issue them to. He's been trained to deal with the civil population, and ends up faced with an awkward devil like you.

John If you've quite finished with compliments, would you pass me the bag by your feet.

Ellie passes him the bag. John opens it and takes out a grenade which he places on the table. He puts the bag on the floor

Ellie (*picking up the grenade*) What on earth is this?

John It's a gas grenade. I picked it up at the Government Research Station where I used to work.

Ellie What is it for?

John When you enter into negotiations with somebody like Evans you have to be very persuasive.

Ellie It certainly looks convincing — is it genuine?

John Oh yes.

Ellie John, I've only known you for a very short time, but I trust you more than I think I've ever trusted anyone. All I ask is that you remember that if the English race has any sort of future at all, it is probably in that bunker. It's a very fragile hope, don't destroy it.

John I won't. I promise.

Ellie (*pouring two more drinks*) And now, let us drink a toast.

John What shall we drink to? The future?

Ellie No . . . No, John, our future was buried with yesterday. Let's drink to the past.

They drink and the Lights fade to Black-out

SCENE 4

The office

The Lights come up on Evans and Martin, leaning over the desk looking at a map. The telephone rings

Evans (*answering the telephone*) Evans here. . . . Right. . . . No, keep him there. Captain Martin will come for him. (*He replaces the receiver*) Ferris has arrived. Will you go and bring him down, please?

Martin Certainly, sir.

Martin exits

Evans folds up the map, tidies some papers on the desk, and places the map and papers in a drawer. He brings a chair and places it on the opposite side of the desk to his own. Then he walks round the desk and sits in his own chair

Captain Martin enters, followed by John

Mr Ferris, sir.

Evans (*standing*) I'm very pleased to meet you at last, Mr Ferris.

Evans holds out his hand, John keeps both hands firmly in his jacket pockets

John No you're not.

There is an awkward pause

Martin I—er—I was just saying to Mr Ferris that I thought I'd met him somewhere before.

Pause

John Mr Evans, Captain Martin, I'm afraid that outside we have ceased to bother with pleasantries and social niceties, and I can see no point to my observing them for the short time that I am in here.

Evans (*coldly*) Very well, at least I suggest we all sit down.

They sit

Now then, Mr Ferris, why did you insist on this meeting?

John I want some questions answered.

Evans I could have done that over the phone.

John I wanted to be sure I was getting the truth.

Evans And what are your questions?

John First of all what went wrong?

Evans I don't follow you.

John All the government propaganda said that there would be millions of survivors—where the hell are they all?

Martin Presumably all the calculations were based on the assumption that there would be only limited nuclear strikes at selected targets. In the event the British Isles appear to have been subject to an initial massive overkill strike. All the major concentrations of population were obliterated in the first few minutes. Any survivors outside the towns died very quickly from the extremely high levels of radiation which existed for about twenty-four hours.

John Do you know of any other survivors?

Evans We did have some radio contact with a Centre just to the north of Carlisle, but it was very garbled, and after thirty-six hours it ceased. We also picked up transmissions from someone near Aberdeen, but he didn't seem able to pick up our broadcasts. The last time he transmitted was about twelve days ago. There may be some others, but unless they've got radio equipment we can't contact them.

John What about Europe?

Martin We've heard nothing at all since the first day. It would seem that the whole of the northern hemisphere has been virtually wiped out.

John (*stunned*) God in heaven.

Evans So you see, Ferris, you people in the village, and we in the Centre, must work together. We need each other.

John Why has the village survived until now?

Pause. Evans and Martin look uncomfortable

Martin We're not really sure.

John You must have some theory.

Martin The first local bomb detonated at ground level on the docks. We also detected two other bombs which detonated harmlessly very high in the atmosphere further up the coast. We think they were probably intended for this Centre and the Government Research Station, but that they exploded prematurely. If either had reached their target the village would have gone as well. Because of the ridge of high ground between the village and the town it would appear that most of the blast, heat, and initial radiation from the bomb which hit the docks was deflected. The prevailing winds took most of the fall-out away from the village.

Evans Yes the radiation levels were much lower in the village than we expected.

John What were the radiation levels?

Pause

Martin The maximum level reached was just over 700 roentgen.

John And what is the lethal level?

Martin It's very difficult to answer that.

John Try.

Martin It varies from person to person, and then there is the time factor to be considered. It really is very difficult to be precise. Doctor Henderson could explain it far better than I.

John Doctor? You've got a doctor in here?

Evans Oh yes. A doctor, a trained nurse, and a fully-equipped sick bay.

John I'd like to speak to your Doctor Henderson.

Evans That won't be necessary, Captain Martin and I will answer all your questions.

John sits slumped in his chair. Eventually he sighs and takes the grenade out of his pocket

John Captain Martin, I presume you know what this is?

Martin Where the hell did you get that from?

John From the Government Chemical Warfare Research Station where I used to be a Chief Technician — and don't try to take it from me, it's already primed.

Martin That's where I'd seen you before.

John Yes. You were there about four months ago on a familiariz- ation course.

Evans Will somebody please explain what is going on?

John This, Mr Evans, is a fairly standard gas grenade. The only modification that I have made is to shorten the fuse to about one second. It is primed, and the only thing stopping it from going off is my thumb which is holding down the trigger mechanism. It contains an advanced form of nerve gas with the code name "Orange Nine".

Martin Christ!

John Perhaps Captain Martin could tell about "Orange Nine"?

Martin According to what we were told four months ago, it is one of the most toxic substances yet developed. The minimum lethal dose has not yet been discovered ... death is virtually in- stantaneous and for that reason nobody knows what it tastes or smells like.

John Excellent! You really did pay attention in class.

Evans Mr Ferris. As the person in charge of this Centre I feel I must warn you——

John (*interrupting*) Captain Martin. You're an intelligent man. In your considered opinion, who is presently in charge of this Centre?

Martin You are.

Evans Have you taken leave of your——

Martin (*interrupting*) Mr Evans, if Mr Ferris were to release that trigger, you and I would die almost immediately. Within a few seconds the gas would have spread throughout the Centre, via the ventilation system, killing everybody else.

Pause

John (*pleasantly*) Well now we understand each other, perhaps you'd pick up the phone and get Doctor Henderson in here.

Evans I shall hold you personally responsible for all this, Captain Martin. My report shall make it quite clear that you failed to ensure the security of the Centre.

Martin Put what you like in your report, but just do as Mr Ferris says.

Evans picks up the telephone and dials a single number

Evans Doctor Henderson? . . . Will you come into my office, please. . . . Yes, immediately. . . . Thank you. (*He replaces the receiver*) You can't possibly get away with this. What do you hope to achieve by this nonsense?

John Captain, Mr Evans is getting on my nerves. If he continues to do so, I shall expect you to render him unconscious by whatever means you deem appropriate. Is that clearly understood?

Martin Yes, sir.

Doctor Henderson enters. The doctor is aged about thirty

John Doctor Henderson, I presume?

Henderson (*unsure of the situation*) That is correct.

John I'm sorry that I don't offer to shake hands, as you can see I've got my hand full at the moment. However, I'm sure that both Mr Evans and Captain Martin will confirm that you should answer all my questions and obey all my instructions.

Doctor Henderson looks at Evans and then Martin

Martin Just do as he says, Doctor.

John Tell me, Doctor, what is the lethal dose of radiation?

Henderson I'm not an expert in that field . . . but it is generally accepted that between 300 and 800 rads will prove to be lethal.

John Rads?

Henderson Radiation absorbed dose.

John So you would expect all the people who were in the village during the twenty-four hours after the attack to die of radiation poisoning?

Henderson I'm surprised they've lived this long.

John I see. In these last few weeks, while you've been treating the odd headache, have you given any thought at all to the people dying out there?

Henderson I wouldn't have been able to cure them.

John But you could have helped them to die.

Henderson I don't see it as part of my job to kill people.

John *Your job! Your job!* What the hell are you talking about? Have you people absolutely no conception at all of what it's like out there? There's no such things as jobs—no laws, no morals, no beliefs—you just do what has to be done . . . Doctor, have you ever watched anyone die of radiation poisoning?

Henderson No.

John Then this is your lucky day, because I am probably this country's greatest living expert in watching people die of radiation poisoning. Can you describe the symptoms?

Henderson Initially there would be nausea, loss of appetite, inflammation of the mouth and throat, and general debility. During the terminal stages there would be vomiting, internal bleeding, pain——

John (*shouting*) No! Not pain, Doctor, not pain—sheer screaming agony—the like of which you can't begin to imagine, not even in your nightmares—the sort of agony that even when they lapse into unconsciousness, just before the end, still they scream.

Pause

(*Almost talking to himself*) When the first two or three died— screaming their way from this world to the next—we didn't really understand what was happening, but I made up my mind that none of my family were going to suffer that way. (*Bitterly*) It was then I found out that not a single person left in the village had any medical knowledge at all—not even first aid. My middle daughter was the first in my family to go down. When I could bear her agony no longer I took a pillow and pressed it hard over her face ... The human instinct for survival is very strong, even through her agony she fought blindly to prevent me, her little hands tearing at my wrists. (*After a pause*) When I had finished I realized that I would not be able to do it that way again. I needed a quicker way, and I found one. I've used it several times since. The last time was this morning. My youngest daughter—Mandy was her name—was the last of all the children. She went down very quickly. One minute she was bright-eyed, intelligent ... a few minutes later she was a screaming, gibbering, mindless ... I took her in my arms, hugged her and kissed her, trying in some way to let her know that I still loved her, and then I put a pistol to her head and pulled the trigger.

Evans Oh my God.

John (*quietly*) Captain Martin, what are the radiation levels like now?

Martin Almost back to normal.

John How many people are there in the Centre?

Martin Sixty-two.

John Doctor, you have got five minutes to get everybody else out of the Centre. They need only take a few personal possessions with them, everything else they'll ever need is outside.

Evans No! This I will not allow. The orders are quite specific on this matter. Nobody is to leave the Centre.

John Captain Martin, shut him up!

Evans How dare you. I am the properly appointed Controller of this Region and I will———

Martin moves behind Evans and renders him unconscious with a single blow behind the ear. Evans slumps over the desk

John Peace, blessed peace. You know, Captain, I get the impression you rather enjoyed that. Well, Doctor, you have your instructions: get everybody out of the Centre immediately.

Doctor Henderson looks at Martin, who nods

Doctor Henderson exits

What's your name, Captain?

Martin John.

John (*smiling*) Well, John, it seems to me that you're going to be in charge for some time. I won't give you much advice although god knows it's going to be difficult for you. By the way, how many women of child-bearing age are there in the Centre?

Martin About twenty-six or seven.

John Well at least somebody showed some sense. I think if you can keep the group together, and survive next winter, you may make it. But you'll have some hard unpleasant decisions to make and you'll have to be ruthless, especially with yourself.

Martin I realize that.

John To begin with, there are forty-three people out there who, during the next few days, are going to die horribly . . . you make sure that bloody doctor of yours overcomes her scruples and does what is necessary — please?

Martin Don't worry. She will.

John One last thing. There's a woman out there called Ellie — I never did learn her other name — tell her that the doctor will take care of my promise to her, and tell her I'll be waiting for her, so there'll be no bitterness or anger.

Martin I'm sorry I don't understand.

John Just tell her. And now you'd better be off yourself. I presume you will be able to close the external doors?

Martin Yes. There's a button just inside the doors with a five-second delay on it.

John You'd better switch off the ventilation system as you leave, I won't be needing it.

Evans groans and starts to move

Martin What about Mr Evans?

John He can keep me company for a little while.

Martin But——

John Out there you are going to be faced with many problems — he would be just one more. Eventually you would have to kill him. You see, I'm taking one of those unpleasant decisions for you. Goodbye, John.

Martin hesitates

Martin (*eventually*) Goodbye.

Martin exits quickly

Evans groans again. John sighs, then walks round the desk and starts patting Evans on the face

John Come on, Mr Evans, time to wake up.

Evans (*sitting up groggily*) What the . . . oooh . . . what on earth . . .? Oh it's you . . . Where's Captain Martin?

John Outside with everyone else.

Evans tries to stand but falls back in his chair

I should stay where you are for a couple of minutes. You're not in any condition to go anywhere.

Evans Why have you done this? You don't even know if they'll be able to survive outside.

John No I don't — but I do know that the longer they stayed in here the more difficult it would be when they eventually went out.

Evans Some of them are little more than school children. How do you think they'll manage?

John They'll either learn, or they'll die. That's the way things are out there. I shouldn't worry too much, the young learn very quickly.

Pause

Did you have any family?

Evans A son in his last year at Cambridge, and a daughter just getting ready to sit her A levels. I've tried not to think of them these last few weeks . . . succeeded most of the time . . . except when I've been alone.

John (*cheerfully*) Well at least you won't have to worry about being alone anymore. You'll be in here with me.

Evans What — what do you mean?

John Just what I say. You'd only be in the way outside, so you're staying here with me.

Evans It's all right for you to say that, you're going to die anyway.

John Wrong, Mr Evans, wrong! When the first attack took place I was three hundred feet underground, pot-holing with two friends. We guessed what had happened. My two friends left immediately and presumably died shortly after reaching the surface. I stayed cowering in the darkness for over four days, consoling myself with the belief that all my family had died

within the first few minutes. Imagine my shame when I found
them still alive. You and I are a sort of sacrifice.

Evans Sacrifice! In God's name what for?

John For the peace of millions of souls who are crying out for
revenge.

Evans Revenge?

John Yes, Mr Evans. Revenge on the scientists who made it
possible, and the politicians who made it inevitable. I'm not
much of a scientist, and you're not much of a politician, but we
are all that is left.

Evans I think you're bluffing.

John (*quietly*) Bluffing?

Evans Yes; about that grenade and all that mumbo-jumbo about
"Orange Nine". Well you don't frighten me, Ferris, do you hear?
You don't frighten me. And now I'll go and see to those idiots
outside. (*He starts to leave*)

John (*sharply*) Mr Evans.

Evans turns

    (*Smiling*) Catch!

*John throws the grenade to Evans, who catches it, and gives a loud
intake of breath*

BLACK-OUT

FURNITURE AND PROPERTY LIST

Please see the Author's Note on page iv concerning the setting. The furniture for John's room and the office should be pre-set and only essential items are listed.

On stage: JOHN'S ROOM
        Table. *On it:* telephone. *Under it:* knapsack containing a
          grenade
        2 chairs

        OFFICE
        Desk. *On it:* telephone and extension, papers, map
        3 chairs

Scene 1

Off stage: Nil

Scene 2

Personal: **John:** pistol in jacket pocket

Scene 3

Off stage: Bottle of whisky, 2 glasses **(Ellie)**

Scene 4

Personal: **John:** grenade in jacket pocket

LIGHTING PLOT

Property fittings required: nil
Various simple interior and exterior settings

SCENE 1

To open: Pool of light on **Vicar** and **John**

Cue 1	**Vicar** stands motionless, head bowed *Slow cross fade to **John**'s room for* SCENE 2	(Page 4)

SCENE 2

Cue 2	**John:** "What do you want?" *Bring up office area lighting*	(Page 4)
Cue 3	**John** slams down telephone receiver *Lighting fades quickly on **John**'s room*	(Page 6)
Cue 4	**Martin:** "To see if Ferris rings back." *Slow cross fade to **John**'s room for* SCENE 3	(Page 7)

SCENE 3

Cue 5	**John** dials single number *Bring up office area lighting*	(Page 9)
Cue 6	**John** replaces receiver *Fade lighting on office area*	(Page 11)
Cue 7	**Ellie** and **John** drink *Fade to Black-out*	(Page 11)

SCENE 4

To open: Office area lit

Cue 8	**Evans** catches grenade with loud intake of breath *Black-out*	(Page 20)

EFFECTS PLOT

MADE AND PRINTED IN GREAT BRITAIN BY
LATIMER TREND & COMPANY LTD PLYMOUTH
MADE IN ENGLAND